Organizer &
Notebook

BARBOUR
PUBLISHING, INC.
Uhrichsville, Ohio

ISBN 1-55748-460-0

Published by Barbour Publishing, Inc.
    P.O. Box 719
    Uhrichsville, Ohio 44683
    http://www.barbourbooks.com

Member of the
Evangelical Christian
Publishers Association

Printed in the United States of America.

Teacher/Speaker _____

Place _____ Date _____
                                           Mo.   Date   Yr.

Title or Subject _____

Book/Chapters/Verses _____

_____

_____

_____

_____

_____

Notes/Outline _____

_____

_____

_____

_____

_____

_____

_____

_____

_____

_____

_____

_____

_____

_____

_____

_____

_____

II TIMOTHY 2:15 — Study to shew thyself approved unto God, a workman
that needeth not to be ashamed, rightly dividing the word of truth.

Notes/Outline Continue

_____
_____
_____
_____
_____
_____
_____
_____
_____
_____
_____
_____
_____
_____
_____
_____
_____

Application: How can I apply this lesson to my personal life?

_____
_____
_____
_____
_____
_____
_____

Teacher/Speaker _____

Place _____ Date _____
                                           Mo.   Date   Yr.

Title or Subject _____

Book/Chapters/Verses _____

_____

_____

_____

_____

_____

Notes/Outline _____

_____

_____

_____

_____

_____

_____

_____

_____

_____

_____

_____

_____

_____

_____

_____

_____

_____

_____

II TIMOTHY 2:15 — Study to shew thyself approved unto God, a workman
that needeth not to be ashamed, rightly dividing the word of truth.

Notes/Outline Continue

_____
_____
_____
_____
_____
_____
_____
_____
_____
_____
_____
_____
_____
_____
_____
_____
_____

Application: How can I apply this lesson to my personal life?

_____
_____
_____
_____
_____
_____
_____
_____

Teacher/Speaker _____

Place _____ **Date** _____
Mo.   Date   Yr.

Title or Subject _____

Book/Chapters/Verses _____

_____

_____

_____

_____

_____

Notes/Outline _____

_____

_____

_____

_____

_____

_____

_____

_____

_____

_____

_____

_____

_____

_____

_____

_____

_____

II TIMOTHY 2:15 — Study to shew thyself approved unto God, a workman
that needeth not to be ashamed, rightly dividing the word of truth.

Notes/Outline Continue

_____

_____

_____

_____

_____

_____

_____

_____

_____

_____

_____

_____

_____

_____

_____

_____

_____

_____

Application: How can I apply this lesson to my personal life?

_____

_____

_____

_____

_____

_____

_____

_____

Teacher/Speaker _____

Place _____ Date _____
                                    Mo.   Date   Yr.

Title or Subject _____

Book/Chapters/Verses _____

_____

_____

_____

_____

_____

Notes/Outline _____

_____

_____

_____

_____

_____

_____

_____

_____

_____

_____

_____

_____

_____

_____

_____

_____

_____

II TIMOTHY 2:15 — Study to shew thyself approved unto God, a workman that needeth not to be ashamed, rightly dividing the word of truth.

Notes/Outline Continue

_____
_____
_____
_____
_____
_____
_____
_____
_____
_____
_____
_____
_____
_____
_____
_____
_____
_____

Application: How can I apply this lesson to my personal life?

_____
_____
_____
_____
_____
_____
_____
_____

Teacher/Speaker _____

Place _____ **Date** _____
Mo.   Date   Yr.

Title or Subject _____

Book/Chapters/Verses _____

_____

_____

_____

_____

_____

Notes/Outline _____

_____

_____

_____

_____

_____

_____

_____

_____

_____

_____

_____

_____

_____

_____

_____

_____

_____

_____

II TIMOTHY 2:15 — Study to shew thyself approved unto God, a workman that needeth not to be ashamed, rightly dividing the word of truth.

Notes/Outline Continue

_____
_____
_____
_____
_____
_____
_____
_____
_____
_____
_____
_____
_____
_____
_____
_____
_____

Application: How can I apply this lesson to my personal life?

_____
_____
_____
_____
_____
_____
_____
_____

Teacher/Speaker _____

Place _____ Date _____
                                              Mo.   Date   Yr.

Title or Subject _____

Book/Chapters/Verses _____

_____

_____

_____

_____

Notes/Outline _____

_____

_____

_____

_____

_____

_____

_____

_____

_____

_____

_____

_____

_____

_____

_____

_____

II TIMOTHY 2:15 — Study to shew thyself approved unto God, a workman
that needeth not to be ashamed, rightly dividing the word of truth.

Notes/Outline Continue

Application: How can I apply this lesson to my personal life?

Teacher/Speaker _____

Place _____ **Date** _____
                                              Mo.   Date   Yr.

Title or Subject _____

Book/Chapters/Verses _____

_____

_____

_____

_____

Notes/Outline _____

_____

_____

_____

_____

_____

_____

_____

_____

_____

_____

_____

_____

_____

_____

_____

_____

_____

_____

II TIMOTHY 2:15 — Study to shew thyself approved unto God, a workman
that needeth not to be ashamed, rightly dividing the word of truth.

Notes/Outline Continue

_____

_____

_____

_____

_____

_____

_____

_____

_____

_____

_____

_____

_____

_____

_____

_____

Application: How can I apply this lesson to my personal life?

_____

_____

_____

_____

_____

_____

_____

Teacher/Speaker _____

Place _____ Date _____
                                        Mo.   Date   Yr.

Title or Subject _____

Book/Chapters/Verses _____

_____
_____
_____
_____
_____

Notes/Outline _____

_____
_____
_____
_____
_____
_____
_____
_____
_____
_____
_____
_____
_____
_____
_____
_____
_____
_____
_____

II TIMOTHY 2:15 — Study to shew thyself approved unto God, a workman
that needeth not to be ashamed, rightly dividing the word of truth.

Notes/Outline Continue

_____

_____

_____

_____

_____

_____

_____

_____

_____

_____

_____

_____

_____

_____

_____

_____

Application: How can I apply this lesson to my personal life?

_____

_____

_____

_____

_____

_____

_____

Teacher/Speaker _____

Place _____ Date _____
                                                Mo.   Date   Yr.

Title or Subject _____

Book/Chapters/Verses _____

_____

_____

_____

_____

_____

Notes/Outline _____

_____

_____

_____

_____

_____

_____

_____

_____

_____

_____

_____

_____

_____

_____

_____

_____

II TIMOTHY 2:15 — Study to shew thyself approved unto God, a workman
that needeth not to be ashamed, rightly dividing the word of truth.

Notes/Outline Continue

_____

_____

_____

_____

_____

_____

_____

_____

_____

_____

_____

_____

_____

_____

_____

_____

_____

Application: How can I apply this lesson to my personal life?

_____

_____

_____

_____

_____

_____

_____

Teacher/Speaker _____

Place _____ Date _____
                                      Mo.   Date   Yr.

Title or Subject _____

Book/Chapters/Verses _____

_____

_____

_____

_____

_____

Notes/Outline _____

_____

_____

_____

_____

_____

_____

_____

_____

_____

_____

_____

_____

_____

_____

_____

_____

_____

II TIMOTHY 2:15 — Study to shew thyself approved unto God, a workman
that needeth not to be ashamed, rightly dividing the word of truth.

Application: How can I apply this lesson to my personal life?

Teacher/Speaker _____

Place _____ Date _____
                                        Mo.   Date   Yr.

Title or Subject _____

Book/Chapters/Verses _____

_____

_____

_____

_____

_____

Notes/Outline _____

_____

_____

_____

_____

_____

_____

_____

_____

_____

_____

_____

_____

_____

_____

_____

_____

_____

_____

_____

II TIMOTHY 2:15 — Study to shew thyself approved unto God, a workman
that needeth not to be ashamed, rightly dividing the word of truth.

Notes/Outline Continue

_____
_____
_____
_____
_____
_____
_____
_____
_____
_____
_____
_____
_____
_____
_____
_____
_____
_____

Application: How can I apply this lesson to my personal life?

_____
_____
_____
_____
_____
_____
_____
_____

Teacher/Speaker _____

Place _____ **Date** _____

Mo.   Date   Yr.

Title or Subject _____

Book/Chapters/Verses _____

_____

_____

_____

_____

Notes/Outline _____

_____

_____

_____

_____

_____

_____

_____

_____

_____

_____

_____

_____

_____

_____

_____

_____

_____

_____

II TIMOTHY 2:15 — Study to shew thyself approved unto God, a workman that needeth not to be ashamed, rightly dividing the word of truth.

_____

_____

_____

_____

_____

_____

_____

_____

_____

_____

_____

_____

_____

_____

_____

_____

_____

_____

Application: How can I apply this lesson to my personal life?

_____

_____

_____

_____

_____

_____

_____

_____

Teacher/Speaker _____

Place _____ Date _____
                                    Mo.   Date   Yr.

Title or Subject _____

Book/Chapters/Verses _____

_____

_____

_____

_____

_____

Notes/Outline

_____

_____

_____

_____

_____

_____

_____

_____

_____

_____

_____

_____

_____

_____

_____

_____

_____

_____

_____

_____

_____

II TIMOTHY 2:15 — Study to shew thyself approved unto God, a workman
that needeth not to be ashamed, rightly dividing the word of truth.

Notes/Outline Continue

_____

_____

_____

_____

_____

_____

_____

_____

_____

_____

_____

_____

_____

_____

_____

_____

_____

_____

Application: How can I apply this lesson to my personal life?

_____

_____

_____

_____

_____

_____

_____

Teacher/Speaker _____

Place _____ Date _____
                                                Mo.   Date   Yr.

Title or Subject _____

Book/Chapters/Verses _____

_____

_____

_____

_____

_____

Notes/Outline _____

_____

_____

_____

_____

_____

_____

_____

_____

_____

_____

_____

_____

_____

_____

_____

_____

_____

_____

II TIMOTHY 2:15 — Study to shew thyself approved unto God, a workman
that needeth not to be ashamed, rightly dividing the word of truth.

Notes/Outline Continue

Application: How can I apply this lesson to my personal life?

Teacher/Speaker _____

Place _____ Date _____
                                              Mo.   Date   Yr.
Title or Subject _____

Book/Chapters/Verses _____

_____

_____

_____

_____

Notes/Outline _____

_____

_____

_____

_____

_____

_____

_____

_____

_____

_____

_____

_____

_____

_____

_____

_____

II TIMOTHY 2:15 — Study to shew thyself approved unto God, a workman
that needeth not to be ashamed, rightly dividing the word of truth.

Notes/Outline Continue

_____

_____

_____

_____

_____

_____

_____

_____

_____

_____

_____

_____

_____

_____

_____

_____

Application: How can I apply this lesson to my personal life?

_____

_____

_____

_____

_____

_____

_____

Teacher/Speaker _____

Place _____ Date _____
                                          Mo.   Date   Yr.

Title or Subject _____

Book/Chapters/Verses _____

_____

_____

_____

_____

_____

Notes/Outline _____

_____

_____

_____

_____

_____

_____

_____

_____

_____

_____

_____

_____

_____

_____

_____

_____

_____

_____

II TIMOTHY 2:15 — Study to shew thyself approved unto God, a workman
that needeth not to be ashamed, rightly dividing the word of truth.

Notes/Outline Continue

_____

_____

_____

_____

_____

_____

_____

_____

_____

_____

_____

_____

_____

_____

_____

_____

Application: How can I apply this lesson to my personal life?

_____

_____

_____

_____

_____

_____

_____

Teacher/Speaker _____

Place _____ Date _____
                                            Mo.   Date   Yr.

Title or Subject _____

Book/Chapters/Verses _____

_____

_____

_____

_____

_____

Notes/Outline _____

_____

_____

_____

_____

_____

_____

_____

_____

_____

_____

_____

_____

_____

_____

_____

_____

_____

_____

II TIMOTHY 2:15 — Study to shew thyself approved unto God, a workman
that needeth not to be ashamed, rightly dividing the word of truth.

Notes/Outline Continue

_____
_____
_____
_____
_____
_____
_____
_____
_____
_____
_____
_____
_____
_____
_____

Application: How can I apply this lesson to my personal life?

_____
_____
_____
_____
_____
_____
_____

Teacher/Speaker _____

Place _____ **Date** _____
                                    Mo.   Date   Yr.

Title or Subject _____

Book/Chapters/Verses _____

_____

_____

_____

_____

_____

Notes/Outline

_____

_____

_____

_____

_____

_____

_____

_____

_____

_____

_____

_____

_____

_____

_____

_____

_____

_____

II TIMOTHY 2:15 — Study to shew thyself approved unto God, a workman
that needeth not to be ashamed, rightly dividing the word of truth.

Notes/Outline Continue

_____
_____
_____
_____
_____
_____
_____
_____
_____
_____
_____
_____
_____
_____
_____
_____

Application: How can I apply this lesson to my personal life?

_____
_____
_____
_____
_____
_____
_____
_____

Teacher/Speaker _____

Place _____ Date _____

Title or Subject _____

Book/Chapters/Verses _____

_____

_____

_____

_____

_____

Notes/Outline

_____

_____

_____

_____

_____

_____

_____

_____

_____

_____

_____

_____

_____

_____

_____

_____

_____

II TIMOTHY 2:15 — Study to shew thyself approved unto God, a workman
that needeth not to be ashamed, rightly dividing the word of truth.

Notes/Outline Continue

_____

_____

_____

_____

_____

_____

_____

_____

_____

_____

_____

_____

_____

_____

Application: How can I apply this lesson to my personal life?

_____

_____

_____

_____

_____

_____

_____

Teacher/Speaker _____

Place _____ Date _____
                                    Mo.   Date   Yr.

Title or Subject _____

Book/Chapters/Verses _____

_____

_____

_____

_____

_____

Notes/Outline _____

_____

_____

_____

_____

_____

_____

_____

_____

_____

_____

_____

_____

_____

_____

_____

_____

_____

_____

II TIMOTHY 2:15 — Study to shew thyself approved unto God, a workman
that needeth not to be ashamed, rightly dividing the word of truth.

Notes/Outline Continue

_____

_____

_____

_____

_____

_____

_____

_____

_____

_____

_____

_____

_____

_____

_____

_____

_____

_____

Application: How can I apply this lesson to my personal life?

_____

_____

_____

_____

_____

_____

_____

_____

Teacher/Speaker _____

Place _____ Date _____
                                          Mo.   Date   Yr.

Title or Subject _____

Book/Chapters/Verses _____

_____

_____

_____

_____

_____

Notes/Outline _____

_____

_____

_____

_____

_____

_____

_____

_____

_____

_____

_____

_____

_____

_____

_____

_____

_____

_____

II TIMOTHY 2:15 — Study to shew thyself approved unto God, a workman
that needeth not to be ashamed, rightly dividing the word of truth.

Notes/Outline Continue

_____
_____
_____
_____
_____
_____
_____
_____
_____
_____
_____
_____
_____
_____
_____
_____
_____

Application: How can I apply this lesson to my personal life?

_____
_____
_____
_____
_____
_____
_____
_____

Teacher/Speaker _____

Place _____ Date _____ _____ _____
                                              Mo.   Date   Yr.

Title or Subject _____

Book/Chapters/Verses _____

_____

_____

_____

_____

_____

_____

Notes/Outline _____

_____

_____

_____

_____

_____

_____

_____

_____

_____

_____

_____

_____

_____

_____

_____

_____

_____

II TIMOTHY 2:15 — Study to shew thyself approved unto God, a workman
that needeth not to be ashamed, rightly dividing the word of truth.

Notes/Outline Continue

_____
_____
_____
_____
_____
_____
_____
_____
_____
_____
_____
_____
_____
_____
_____
_____
_____
_____

Application: How can I apply this lesson to my personal life?

_____
_____
_____
_____
_____
_____
_____
_____

Teacher/Speaker _____

Place _____ Date _____
                                        Mo.   Date   Yr.

Title or Subject _____

Book/Chapters/Verses _____

_____

_____

_____

_____

_____

Notes/Outline

_____

_____

_____

_____

_____

_____

_____

_____

_____

_____

_____

_____

_____

_____

_____

_____

_____

II TIMOTHY 2:15 — Study to shew thyself approved unto God, a workman
that needeth not to be ashamed, rightly dividing the word of truth.

Notes/Outline Continue

Application: How can I apply this lesson to my personal life?

Teacher/Speaker _____

Place _____ **Date** _____
                                            Mo.   Date   Yr.

Title or Subject _____

Book/Chapters/Verses _____

_____

_____

_____

_____

Notes/Outline _____

_____

_____

_____

_____

_____

_____

_____

_____

_____

_____

_____

_____

_____

_____

_____

_____

_____

_____

II TIMOTHY 2:15 — Study to shew thyself approved unto God, a workman
that needeth not to be ashamed, rightly dividing the word of truth.

Notes/Outline Continue

Application: How can I apply this lesson to my personal life?

Teacher/Speaker _____

Place _____ Date _____
                                         Mo.   Date   Yr.

Title or Subject _____

Book/Chapters/Verses _____

_____

_____

_____

_____

Notes/Outline

_____

_____

_____

_____

_____

_____

_____

_____

_____

_____

_____

_____

_____

_____

_____

_____

_____

II TIMOTHY 2:15 — Study to shew thyself approved unto God, a workman
that needeth not to be ashamed, rightly dividing the word of truth.

Notes/Outline Continue

_____
_____
_____
_____
_____
_____
_____
_____
_____
_____
_____
_____
_____
_____
_____
_____
_____

Application: How can I apply this lesson to my personal life?

_____
_____
_____
_____
_____
_____
_____
_____

Teacher/Speaker _____

Place _____ Date _____
                                    Mo.   Date   Yr.

Title or Subject _____

Book/Chapters/Verses _____

_____
_____
_____
_____
_____

Notes/Outline _____

_____
_____
_____
_____
_____
_____
_____
_____
_____
_____
_____
_____
_____
_____
_____
_____
_____
_____

II TIMOTHY 2:15 — Study to shew thyself approved unto God, a workman
that needeth not to be ashamed, rightly dividing the word of truth.

Notes/Outline Continue

Application: How can I apply this lesson to my personal life?

Teacher/Speaker _____

Place _____ Date _____
                                           Mo.   Date   Yr.

Title or Subject _____

Book/Chapters/Verses _____

_____

_____

_____

_____

_____

Notes/Outline

_____

_____

_____

_____

_____

_____

_____

_____

_____

_____

_____

_____

_____

_____

_____

_____

_____

_____

_____

II TIMOTHY 2:15 — Study to shew thyself approved unto God, a workman
that needeth not to be ashamed, rightly dividing the word of truth.

Notes/Outline Continue

_____

_____

_____

_____

_____

_____

_____

_____

_____

_____

_____

_____

_____

_____

_____

_____

_____

Application: How can I apply this lesson to my personal life?

_____

_____

_____

_____

_____

_____

_____

_____

Teacher/Speaker _____

Place _____ Date _____
                                  Mo.   Date   Yr.

Title or Subject _____

Book/Chapters/Verses _____

_____

_____

_____

_____

_____

Notes/Outline _____

_____

_____

_____

_____

_____

_____

_____

_____

_____

_____

_____

_____

_____

_____

_____

_____

_____

_____

II TIMOTHY 2:15 — Study to shew thyself approved unto God, a workman
that needeth not to be ashamed, rightly dividing the word of truth.

Notes/Outline Continue

_____
_____
_____
_____
_____
_____
_____
_____
_____
_____
_____
_____
_____
_____
_____
_____
_____

Application: How can I apply this lesson to my personal life?

_____
_____
_____
_____
_____
_____
_____
_____

Teacher/Speaker _____

Place _____ Date _____
                                              Mo.   Date   Yr.

Title or Subject _____

Book/Chapters/Verses _____

_____

_____

_____

_____

_____

Notes/Outline _____

_____

_____

_____

_____

_____

_____

_____

_____

_____

_____

_____

_____

_____

_____

_____

_____

_____

_____

_____

_____

II TIMOTHY 2:15 — Study to shew thyself approved unto God, a workman
that needeth not to be ashamed, rightly dividing the word of truth.

Notes/Outline Continue

_____
_____
_____
_____
_____
_____
_____
_____
_____
_____
_____
_____
_____
_____
_____
_____
_____

Application: How can I apply this lesson to my personal life?

_____
_____
_____
_____
_____
_____
_____
_____

Teacher/Speaker _____

Place _____ Date _____
                                              Mo.   Date   Yr.

Title or Subject _____

Book/Chapters/Verses _____

_____
_____
_____
_____
_____

Notes/Outline _____

_____
_____
_____
_____
_____
_____
_____
_____
_____
_____
_____
_____
_____
_____
_____
_____
_____
_____
_____
_____
_____

II TIMOTHY 2:15 — Study to shew thyself approved unto God, a workman
that needeth not to be ashamed, rightly dividing the word of truth.

Notes/Outline Continue

_____
_____
_____
_____
_____
_____
_____
_____
_____
_____
_____
_____
_____
_____
_____
_____
_____

Application: How can I apply this lesson to my personal life?

_____
_____
_____
_____
_____
_____
_____
_____

Teacher/Speaker _____

Place _____ Date _____
                                                    Mo.   Date   Yr.

Title or Subject _____

Book/Chapters/Verses _____

_____

_____

_____

_____

_____

Notes/Outline

_____

_____

_____

_____

_____

_____

_____

_____

_____

_____

_____

_____

_____

_____

_____

_____

_____

II TIMOTHY 2:15 — Study to shew thyself approved unto God, a workman that needeth not to be ashamed, rightly dividing the word of truth.

Notes/Outline Continue

_____

_____

_____

_____

_____

_____

_____

_____

_____

_____

_____

_____

_____

_____

_____

_____

_____

Application: How can I apply this lesson to my personal life?

_____

_____

_____

_____

_____

_____

_____

_____

Teacher/Speaker _____

Place _____ Date _____
                                        Mo.   Date   Yr.

Title or Subject _____

Book/Chapters/Verses _____

_____

_____

_____

_____

_____

Notes/Outline _____

_____

_____

_____

_____

_____

_____

_____

_____

_____

_____

_____

_____

_____

_____

_____

_____

_____

II TIMOTHY 2:15 — Study to shew thyself approved unto God, a workman
that needeth not to be ashamed, rightly dividing the word of truth.

Notes/Outline Continue

_____

_____

_____

_____

_____

_____

_____

_____

_____

_____

_____

_____

_____

_____

_____

_____

_____

Application: How can I apply this lesson to my personal life?

_____

_____

_____

_____

_____

_____

_____

Teacher/Speaker _____

Place _____ **Date** _____
Mo. Date Yr.

Title or Subject _____

Book/Chapters/Verses _____

_____

_____

_____

_____

_____

Notes/Outline _____

_____

_____

_____

_____

_____

_____

_____

_____

_____

_____

_____

_____

_____

_____

_____

_____

II TIMOTHY 2:15 — Study to shew thyself approved unto God, a workman
that needeth not to be ashamed, rightly dividing the word of truth.

Notes/Outline Continue

Application: How can I apply this lesson to my personal life?

Teacher/Speaker _____

Place _____ Date _____
                                    Mo.   Date   Yr.
Title or Subject _____

Book/Chapters/Verses _____

_____

_____

_____

_____

_____

Notes/Outline _____

_____

_____

_____

_____

_____

_____

_____

_____

_____

_____

_____

_____

_____

_____

_____

_____

_____

_____

_____

II TIMOTHY 2:15 — Study to shew thyself approved unto God, a workman
that needeth not to be ashamed, rightly dividing the word of truth.

Notes/Outline Continue

_____
_____
_____
_____
_____
_____
_____
_____
_____
_____
_____
_____
_____
_____
_____
_____
_____
_____

Application: How can I apply this lesson to my personal life?

_____
_____
_____
_____
_____
_____
_____
_____

Teacher/Speaker _____

Place _____ Date _____
                                    Mo.   Date   Yr.

Title or Subject _____

Book/Chapters/Verses _____

_____
_____
_____
_____
_____

Notes/Outline _____

_____
_____
_____
_____
_____
_____
_____
_____
_____
_____
_____
_____
_____
_____
_____
_____
_____
_____
_____

II TIMOTHY 2:15 — Study to shew thyself approved unto God, a workman
that needeth not to be ashamed, rightly dividing the word of truth.

Notes/Outline Continue

_____
_____
_____
_____
_____
_____
_____
_____
_____
_____
_____
_____
_____
_____
_____
_____

Application: How can I apply this lesson to my personal life?

_____
_____
_____
_____
_____
_____
_____

Teacher/Speaker _____

Place _____ **Date** _____
Mo.   Date   Yr.

Title or Subject _____

Book/Chapters/Verses _____

_____

_____

_____

_____

Notes/Outline _____

_____

_____

_____

_____

_____

_____

_____

_____

_____

_____

_____

_____

_____

_____

_____

_____

_____

II TIMOTHY 2:15 — Study to shew thyself approved unto God, a workman
that needeth not to be ashamed, rightly dividing the word of truth.

Notes/Outline Continue

_____

_____

_____

_____

_____

_____

_____

_____

_____

_____

_____

_____

_____

_____

_____

_____

Application: How can I apply this lesson to my personal life?

_____

_____

_____

_____

_____

_____

_____

Teacher/Speaker _____

Place _____ **Date** _____
                   Mo.   Date   Yr.

Title or Subject _____

Book/Chapters/Verses _____

_____
_____
_____
_____
_____

Notes/Outline _____

_____
_____
_____
_____
_____
_____
_____
_____
_____
_____
_____
_____
_____
_____
_____
_____
_____
_____
_____
_____
_____

II TIMOTHY 2:15 — Study to shew thyself approved unto God, a workman
that needeth not to be ashamed, rightly dividing the word of truth.

Notes/Outline Continue

_____
_____
_____
_____
_____
_____
_____
_____
_____
_____
_____
_____
_____
_____
_____
_____

Application: How can I apply this lesson to my personal life?

_____
_____
_____
_____
_____
_____
_____

Teacher/Speaker _____

Place _____ Date _____
                                        Mo.   Date   Yr.

Title or Subject _____

Book/Chapters/Verses _____

_____

_____

_____

_____

_____

Notes/Outline _____

_____

_____

_____

_____

_____

_____

_____

_____

_____

_____

_____

_____

_____

_____

_____

_____

_____

II TIMOTHY 2:15 — Study to shew thyself approved unto God, a workman
that needeth not to be ashamed, rightly dividing the word of truth.

Notes/Outline Continue

_____

_____

_____

_____

_____

_____

_____

_____

_____

_____

_____

_____

_____

_____

_____

Application: How can I apply this lesson to my personal life?

_____

_____

_____

_____

_____

_____

_____

_____

Teacher/Speaker _____

Place _____ **Date** _____
Mo.   Date   Yr.

Title or Subject _____

Book/Chapters/Verses _____

_____

_____

_____

_____

_____

Notes/Outline

_____

_____

_____

_____

_____

_____

_____

_____

_____

_____

_____

_____

_____

_____

_____

_____

_____

_____

II TIMOTHY 2:15 — Study to shew thyself approved unto God, a workman
that needeth not to be ashamed, rightly dividing the word of truth.

Notes/Outline Continue

_____

_____

_____

_____

_____

_____

_____

_____

_____

_____

_____

_____

_____

_____

_____

_____

_____

Application: How can I apply this lesson to my personal life?

_____

_____

_____

_____

_____

_____

_____

_____

_____

Teacher/Speaker _____

Place _____ Date _____
                                        Mo.   Date   Yr.

Title or Subject _____

Book/Chapters/Verses _____

_____

_____

_____

_____

_____

Notes/Outline _____

_____

_____

_____

_____

_____

_____

_____

_____

_____

_____

_____

_____

_____

_____

_____

_____

_____

_____

II TIMOTHY 2:15 — Study to shew thyself approved unto God, a workman
that needeth not to be ashamed, rightly dividing the word of truth.

Notes/Outline Continue

_____

_____

_____

_____

_____

_____

_____

_____

_____

_____

_____

_____

_____

_____

_____

_____

_____

Application: How can I apply this lesson to my personal life?

_____

_____

_____

_____

_____

_____

_____

Teacher/Speaker _____

Place _____ Date _____
                                              Mo.   Date   Yr.

Title or Subject _____

Book/Chapters/Verses _____

_____

_____

_____

_____

_____

Notes/Outline

_____

_____

_____

_____

_____

_____

_____

_____

_____

_____

_____

_____

_____

_____

_____

_____

_____

_____

II TIMOTHY 2:15 — Study to shew thyself approved unto God, a workman
that needeth not to be ashamed, rightly dividing the word of truth.

Notes/Outline Continue

_____
_____
_____
_____
_____
_____
_____
_____
_____
_____
_____
_____
_____
_____
_____
_____

Application: How can I apply this lesson to my personal life?

_____
_____
_____
_____
_____
_____
_____

Teacher/Speaker _____

Place _____ Date _____
                                                Mo.   Date   Yr.

Title or Subject _____

Book/Chapters/Verses _____

_____

_____

_____

_____

Notes/Outline _____

_____

_____

_____

_____

_____

_____

_____

_____

_____

_____

_____

_____

_____

_____

_____

_____

II TIMOTHY 2:15 — Study to shew thyself approved unto God, a workman
that needeth not to be ashamed, rightly dividing the word of truth.

Notes/Outline Continue

_____

_____

_____

_____

_____

_____

_____

_____

_____

_____

_____

_____

_____

_____

_____

_____

_____

_____

Application: How can I apply this lesson to my personal life?

_____

_____

_____

_____

_____

_____

_____

_____

Teacher/Speaker _____

Place _____ **Date** _____
                                    Mo.   Date   Yr.

Title or Subject _____

Book/Chapters/Verses _____

_____
_____
_____
_____
_____

Notes/Outline _____

_____
_____
_____
_____
_____
_____
_____
_____
_____
_____
_____
_____
_____
_____
_____
_____
_____
_____
_____
_____

II TIMOTHY 2:15 — Study to shew thyself approved unto God, a workman
that needeth not to be ashamed, rightly dividing the word of truth.

Notes/Outline Continue

_____
_____
_____
_____
_____
_____
_____
_____
_____
_____
_____
_____
_____
_____
_____
_____
_____
_____

Application: How can I apply this lesson to my personal life?

_____
_____
_____
_____
_____
_____
_____
_____

Teacher/Speaker _____

Place _____ Date _____
Mo.   Date   Yr.

Title or Subject _____

Book/Chapters/Verses _____

_____

_____

_____

_____

_____

Notes/Outline _____

_____

_____

_____

_____

_____

_____

_____

_____

_____

_____

_____

_____

_____

_____

_____

_____

_____

_____

II TIMOTHY 2:15 — Study to shew thyself approved unto God, a workman
that needeth not to be ashamed, rightly dividing the word of truth.

Notes/Outline Continue

_____
_____
_____
_____
_____
_____
_____
_____
_____
_____
_____
_____
_____
_____
_____

Application: How can I apply this lesson to my personal life?

_____
_____
_____
_____
_____
_____
_____

Teacher/Speaker _____

Place _____ **Date** _____
Mo.   Date   Yr.

Title or Subject _____

Book/Chapters/Verses _____

_____

_____

_____

_____

_____

Notes/Outline _____

_____

_____

_____

_____

_____

_____

_____

_____

_____

_____

_____

_____

_____

_____

_____

_____

_____

_____

II TIMOTHY 2:15 — Study to shew thyself approved unto God, a workman that needeth not to be ashamed, rightly dividing the word of truth.

Notes/Outline Continue

_____
_____
_____
_____
_____
_____
_____
_____
_____
_____
_____
_____
_____
_____
_____
_____
_____
_____

Application: How can I apply this lesson to my personal life?

_____
_____
_____
_____
_____
_____
_____
_____
_____

Teacher/Speaker _____

Place _____ Date _____

Mo.   Date   Yr.

Title or Subject _____

Book/Chapters/Verses _____

_____

_____

_____

_____

Notes/Outline _____

_____

_____

_____

_____

_____

_____

_____

_____

_____

_____

_____

_____

_____

_____

_____

_____

_____

II TIMOTHY 2:15 — Study to shew thyself approved unto God, a workman
that needeth not to be ashamed, rightly dividing the word of truth.

Notes/Outline Continue

_____
_____
_____
_____
_____
_____
_____
_____
_____
_____
_____
_____
_____
_____
_____

Application: How can I apply this lesson to my personal life?

_____
_____
_____
_____
_____
_____
_____

Teacher/Speaker _____

Place _____ Date _____
                                                 Mo.   Date   Yr.

Title or Subject _____

Book/Chapters/Verses _____

_____

_____

_____

_____

_____

Notes/Outline _____

_____

_____

_____

_____

_____

_____

_____

_____

_____

_____

_____

_____

_____

_____

_____

_____

_____

II TIMOTHY 2:15 — Study to shew thyself approved unto God, a workman
that needeth not to be ashamed, rightly dividing the word of truth.

Notes/Outline Continue

Application: How can I apply this lesson to my personal life?